This music practice diary belongs to

....

Manuscript

Lesson Notes

Lesson date:

In our lesson today, we worked on the following:

Key things to practise this week
Exercises/Scales:

Pieces:

Other important areas of focus including: Sight-reading, Music Theory, Aural, Listening

The boxes below are to record the number of minutes practice you do each day:

Monday	Tuesday	Wednesday	Thursday	Friday	Saturday	Sunday

Manuscript

Lesson Notes

Lesson date:

In our lesson today, we worked on the following:

Key things to practise this week
Exercises/Scales:

Pieces:

Other important areas of focus including: Sight-reading, Music Theory, Aural, Listening

The boxes below are to record the number of minutes practice you do each day:

Monday	Tuesday	Wednesday	Thursday	Friday	Saturday	Sunday

Manuscript

Lesson Notes

Lesson date:

In our lesson today, we worked on the following:

Key things to practise this week
Exercises/Scales:

Pieces:

Other important areas of focus including: Sight-reading, Music Theory, Aural, Listening

The boxes below are to record the number of minutes practice you do each day:

Monday	Tuesday	Wednesday	Thursday	Friday	Saturday	Sunday

Manuscript

Lesson Notes

Lesson date:

In our lesson today, we worked on the following:

Key things to practise this week
Exercises/Scales:

Pieces:

Other important areas of focus including: Sight-reading, Music Theory, Aural, Listening

The boxes below are to record the number of minutes practice you do each day:

Monday	Tuesday	Wednesday	Thursday	Friday	Saturday	Sunday

Manuscript

Lesson Notes

Lesson date:

In our lesson today, we worked on the following:

Key things to practise this week
Exercises/Scales:

Pieces:

Other important areas of focus including: Sight-reading, Music Theory, Aural, Listening

The boxes below are to record the number of minutes practice you do each day:

Monday	Tuesday	Wednesday	Thursday	Friday	Saturday	Sunday

Manuscript

Lesson Notes

Lesson date:

In our lesson today, we worked on the following:

Key things to practise this week
Exercises/Scales:

Pieces:

Other important areas of focus including: Sight-reading, Music Theory, Aural, Listening

The boxes below are to record the number of minutes practice you do each day:

Monday	Tuesday	Wednesday	Thursday	Friday	Saturday	Sunday

Lesson Notes

Lesson date:

In our lesson today, we worked on the following:

Key things to practise this week
Exercises/Scales:

Pieces:

Other important areas of focus including: Sight-reading, Music Theory, Aural, Listening

The boxes below are to record the number of minutes practice you do each day:

Monday	Tuesday	Wednesday	Thursday	Friday	Saturday	Sunday

Manuscript

Lesson Notes

Lesson date:

In our lesson today, we worked on the following:

Key things to practise this week
Exercises/Scales:

Pieces:

Other important areas of focus including: Sight-reading, Music Theory, Aural, Listening

The boxes below are to record the number of minutes practice you do each day:

Monday	Tuesday	Wednesday	Thursday	Friday	Saturday	Sunday

Manuscript

Lesson Notes

Lesson date:

In our lesson today, we worked on the following:

Key things to practise this week
Exercises/Scales:

Pieces:

Other important areas of focus including: Sight-reading, Music Theory, Aural, Listening

The boxes below are to record the number of minutes practice you do each day:

Monday	Tuesday	Wednesday	Thursday	Friday	Saturday	Sunday

Manuscript

Lesson Notes

Lesson date:

In our lesson today, we worked on the following:

Key things to practise this week
Exercises/Scales:

Pieces:

Other important areas of focus including: Sight-reading, Music Theory, Aural, Listening

The boxes below are to record the number of minutes practice you do each day:

Monday	Tuesday	Wednesday	Thursday	Friday	Saturday	Sunday

Manuscript

Lesson Notes

Lesson date:

In our lesson today, we worked on the following:

Key things to practise this week
Exercises/Scales:

Pieces:

Other important areas of focus including: Sight-reading, Music Theory, Aural, Listening

The boxes below are to record the number of minutes practice you do each day:

Monday	Tuesday	Wednesday	Thursday	Friday	Saturday	Sunday

Lesson Notes

Lesson date:

In our lesson today, we worked on the following:

Key things to practise this week
Exercises/Scales:

Pieces:

Other important areas of focus including: Sight-reading, Music Theory, Aural, Listening

The boxes below are to record the number of minutes practice you do each day:

Monday	Tuesday	Wednesday	Thursday	Friday	Saturday	Sunday

Manuscript

Lesson Notes

Lesson date:

In our lesson today, we worked on the following:

Key things to practise this week
Exercises/Scales:

Pieces:

Other important areas of focus including: Sight-reading, Music Theory, Aural, Listening

The boxes below are to record the number of minutes practice you do each day:

Monday	Tuesday	Wednesday	Thursday	Friday	Saturday	Sunday

Manuscript

Lesson Notes

Lesson date:

In our lesson today, we worked on the following:

Key things to practise this week
Exercises/Scales:

Pieces:

Other important areas of focus including: Sight-reading, Music Theory, Aural, Listening

The boxes below are to record the number of minutes practice you do each day:

Monday	Tuesday	Wednesday	Thursday	Friday	Saturday	Sunday

Lesson Notes

Lesson date:

In our lesson today, we worked on the following:

Key things to practise this week
Exercises/Scales:

Pieces:

Other important areas of focus including: Sight-reading, Music Theory, Aural, Listening

The boxes below are to record the number of minutes practice you do each day:

Monday	Tuesday	Wednesday	Thursday	Friday	Saturday	Sunday

Manuscript

Lesson Notes

Lesson date:

In our lesson today, we worked on the following:

Key things to practise this week
Exercises/Scales:

Pieces:

Other important areas of focus including: Sight-reading, Music Theory, Aural, Listening

The boxes below are to record the number of minutes practice you do each day:

Monday	Tuesday	Wednesday	Thursday	Friday	Saturday	Sunday

Lesson Notes

Lesson date:

In our lesson today, we worked on the following:

Key things to practise this week
Exercises/Scales:

Pieces:

Other important areas of focus including: Sight-reading, Music Theory, Aural, Listening

The boxes below are to record the number of minutes practice you do each day:

Monday	Tuesday	Wednesday	Thursday	Friday	Saturday	Sunday

Manuscript

Lesson Notes

Lesson date:

In our lesson today, we worked on the following:

Key things to practise this week
Exercises/Scales:

Pieces:

Other important areas of focus including: Sight-reading, Music Theory, Aural, Listening

The boxes below are to record the number of minutes practice you do each day:

Monday	Tuesday	Wednesday	Thursday	Friday	Saturday	Sunday

Lesson Notes

Lesson date:

In our lesson today, we worked on the following:

Key things to practise this week
Exercises/Scales:

Pieces:

Other important areas of focus including: Sight-reading, Music Theory, Aural, Listening

The boxes below are to record the number of minutes practice you do each day:

Monday	Tuesday	Wednesday	Thursday	Friday	Saturday	Sunday

Manuscript

Lesson Notes

Lesson date:

In our lesson today, we worked on the following:

Key things to practise this week
Exercises/Scales:

Pieces:

Other important areas of focus including: Sight-reading, Music Theory, Aural, Listening

The boxes below are to record the number of minutes practice you do each day:

Monday	Tuesday	Wednesday	Thursday	Friday	Saturday	Sunday

Lesson Notes

Lesson date:

In our lesson today, we worked on the following:

Key things to practise this week
Exercises/Scales:

Pieces:

Other important areas of focus including: Sight-reading, Music Theory, Aural, Listening

The boxes below are to record the number of minutes practice you do each day:

Monday	Tuesday	Wednesday	Thursday	Friday	Saturday	Sunday

Manuscript

Lesson Notes

Lesson date:

In our lesson today, we worked on the following:

Key things to practise this week
Exercises/Scales:

Pieces:

Other important areas of focus including: Sight-reading, Music Theory, Aural, Listening

The boxes below are to record the number of minutes practice you do each day:

Monday	Tuesday	Wednesday	Thursday	Friday	Saturday	Sunday

Manuscript

Lesson Notes

Lesson date:

In our lesson today, we worked on the following:

Key things to practise this week
Exercises/Scales:

Pieces:

Other important areas of focus including: Sight-reading, Music Theory, Aural, Listening

The boxes below are to record the number of minutes practice you do each day:

Monday	Tuesday	Wednesday	Thursday	Friday	Saturday	Sunday

Lesson Notes

Lesson date:

In our lesson today, we worked on the following:

Key things to practise this week
Exercises/Scales:

Pieces:

Other important areas of focus including: Sight-reading, Music Theory, Aural, Listening

The boxes below are to record the number of minutes practice you do each day:

Monday	Tuesday	Wednesday	Thursday	Friday	Saturday	Sunday

Manuscript

Lesson Notes

Lesson date:

In our lesson today, we worked on the following:

Key things to practise this week
Exercises/Scales:

Pieces:

Other important areas of focus including: Sight-reading, Music Theory, Aural, Listening

The boxes below are to record the number of minutes practice you do each day:

Monday	Tuesday	Wednesday	Thursday	Friday	Saturday	Sunday

Manuscript

Lesson Notes

Lesson date:

In our lesson today, we worked on the following:

Key things to practise this week
Exercises/Scales:

Pieces:

Other important areas of focus including: Sight-reading, Music Theory, Aural, Listening

The boxes below are to record the number of minutes practice you do each day:

Monday	Tuesday	Wednesday	Thursday	Friday	Saturday	Sunday

Lesson Notes

Lesson date:

In our lesson today, we worked on the following:

Key things to practise this week
Exercises/Scales:

Pieces:

Other important areas of focus including: Sight-reading, Music Theory, Aural, Listening

The boxes below are to record the number of minutes practice you do each day:

Monday	Tuesday	Wednesday	Thursday	Friday	Saturday	Sunday

Manuscript

Lesson Notes

Lesson date:

In our lesson today, we worked on the following:

Key things to practise this week
Exercises/Scales:

Pieces:

Other important areas of focus including: Sight-reading, Music Theory, Aural, Listening

The boxes below are to record the number of minutes practice you do each day:

Monday	Tuesday	Wednesday	Thursday	Friday	Saturday	Sunday

Lesson Notes

Lesson date:

In our lesson today, we worked on the following:

Key things to practise this week
Exercises/Scales:

Pieces:

Other important areas of focus including: Sight-reading, Music Theory, Aural, Listening

The boxes below are to record the number of minutes practice you do each day:

Monday	Tuesday	Wednesday	Thursday	Friday	Saturday	Sunday

Lesson Notes

Lesson date:

In our lesson today, we worked on the following:

Key things to practise this week
Exercises/Scales:

Pieces:

Other important areas of focus including: Sight-reading, Music Theory, Aural, Listening

The boxes below are to record the number of minutes practice you do each day:

Monday	Tuesday	Wednesday	Thursday	Friday	Saturday	Sunday

Manuscript

Lesson Notes

Lesson date:

In our lesson today, we worked on the following:

Key things to practise this week
Exercises/Scales:

Pieces:

Other important areas of focus including: Sight-reading, Music Theory, Aural, Listening

The boxes below are to record the number of minutes practice you do each day:

Monday	Tuesday	Wednesday	Thursday	Friday	Saturday	Sunday

Manuscript

Lesson Notes

Lesson date:

In our lesson today, we worked on the following:

Key things to practise this week
Exercises/Scales:

Pieces:

Other important areas of focus including: Sight-reading, Music Theory, Aural, Listening

The boxes below are to record the number of minutes practice you do each day:

Monday	Tuesday	Wednesday	Thursday	Friday	Saturday	Sunday

Lesson Notes

Lesson date:

In our lesson today, we worked on the following:

Key things to practise this week
Exercises/Scales:

Pieces:

Other important areas of focus including: Sight-reading, Music Theory, Aural, Listening

The boxes below are to record the number of minutes practice you do each day:

Monday	Tuesday	Wednesday	Thursday	Friday	Saturday	Sunday

Manuscript

Lesson Notes

Lesson date:

In our lesson today, we worked on the following:

Key things to practise this week
Exercises/Scales:

Pieces:

Other important areas of focus including: Sight-reading, Music Theory, Aural, Listening

The boxes below are to record the number of minutes practice you do each day:

Monday	Tuesday	Wednesday	Thursday	Friday	Saturday	Sunday

Lesson Notes

Lesson date:

In our lesson today, we worked on the following:

Key things to practise this week
Exercises/Scales:

Pieces:

Other important areas of focus including: Sight-reading, Music Theory, Aural, Listening

The boxes below are to record the number of minutes practice you do each day:

Monday	Tuesday	Wednesday	Thursday	Friday	Saturday	Sunday

Manuscript

Lesson Notes

Lesson date:

In our lesson today, we worked on the following:

Key things to practise this week
Exercises/Scales:

Pieces:

Other important areas of focus including: Sight-reading, Music Theory, Aural, Listening

The boxes below are to record the number of minutes practice you do each day:

Monday	Tuesday	Wednesday	Thursday	Friday	Saturday	Sunday

Lesson Notes

Lesson date:

In our lesson today, we worked on the following:

Key things to practise this week
Exercises/Scales:

Pieces:

Other important areas of focus including: Sight-reading, Music Theory, Aural, Listening

The boxes below are to record the number of minutes practice you do each day:

Monday	Tuesday	Wednesday	Thursday	Friday	Saturday	Sunday

Lesson Notes

Lesson date:

In our lesson today, we worked on the following:

Key things to practise this week
Exercises/Scales:

Pieces:

Other important areas of focus including: Sight-reading, Music Theory, Aural, Listening

The boxes below are to record the number of minutes practice you do each day:

Monday	Tuesday	Wednesday	Thursday	Friday	Saturday	Sunday

Lesson Notes

Lesson date:

In our lesson today, we worked on the following:

Key things to practise this week
Exercises/Scales:

Pieces:

Other important areas of focus including: Sight-reading, Music Theory, Aural, Listening

The boxes below are to record the number of minutes practice you do each day:

Monday	Tuesday	Wednesday	Thursday	Friday	Saturday	Sunday

Lesson Notes

Lesson date:

In our lesson today, we worked on the following:

Key things to practise this week
Exercises/Scales:

Pieces:

Other important areas of focus including: Sight-reading, Music Theory, Aural, Listening

The boxes below are to record the number of minutes practice you do each day:

Monday	Tuesday	Wednesday	Thursday	Friday	Saturday	Sunday

Manuscript

Lesson Notes

Lesson date:

In our lesson today, we worked on the following:

Key things to practise this week
Exercises/Scales:

Pieces:

Other important areas of focus including: Sight-reading, Music Theory, Aural, Listening

The boxes below are to record the number of minutes practice you do each day:

Monday	Tuesday	Wednesday	Thursday	Friday	Saturday	Sunday

Lesson Notes

Lesson date:

In our lesson today, we worked on the following:

Key things to practise this week
Exercises/Scales:

Pieces:

Other important areas of focus including: Sight-reading, Music Theory, Aural, Listening

The boxes below are to record the number of minutes practice you do each day:

Monday	Tuesday	Wednesday	Thursday	Friday	Saturday	Sunday

Lesson Notes

Lesson date:

In our lesson today, we worked on the following:

Key things to practise this week
Exercises/Scales:

Pieces:

Other important areas of focus including: Sight-reading, Music Theory, Aural, Listening

The boxes below are to record the number of minutes practice you do each day:

Monday	Tuesday	Wednesday	Thursday	Friday	Saturday	Sunday

Lesson Notes

Lesson date:

In our lesson today, we worked on the following:

Key things to practise this week
Exercises/Scales:

Pieces:

Other important areas of focus including: Sight-reading, Music Theory, Aural, Listening

The boxes below are to record the number of minutes practice you do each day:

Monday	Tuesday	Wednesday	Thursday	Friday	Saturday	Sunday

Lesson Notes

Lesson date:

In our lesson today, we worked on the following:

Key things to practise this week
Exercises/Scales:

Pieces:

Other important areas of focus including: Sight-reading, Music Theory, Aural, Listening

The boxes below are to record the number of minutes practice you do each day:

Monday	Tuesday	Wednesday	Thursday	Friday	Saturday	Sunday

Lesson Notes

Lesson date:

In our lesson today, we worked on the following:

Key things to practise this week
Exercises/Scales:

Pieces:

Other important areas of focus including: Sight-reading, Music Theory, Aural, Listening

The boxes below are to record the number of minutes practice you do each day:

Monday	Tuesday	Wednesday	Thursday	Friday	Saturday	Sunday

Lesson Notes

Lesson date:

In our lesson today, we worked on the following:

Key things to practise this week
Exercises/Scales:

Pieces:

Other important areas of focus including: Sight-reading, Music Theory, Aural, Listening

The boxes below are to record the number of minutes practice you do each day:

Monday	Tuesday	Wednesday	Thursday	Friday	Saturday	Sunday

Manuscript

Lesson Notes

Lesson date:

In our lesson today, we worked on the following:

Key things to practise this week
Exercises/Scales:

Pieces:

Other important areas of focus including: Sight-reading, Music Theory, Aural, Listening

The boxes below are to record the number of minutes practice you do each day:

Monday	Tuesday	Wednesday	Thursday	Friday	Saturday	Sunday

Lesson Notes

Lesson date:

In our lesson today, we worked on the following:

Key things to practise this week
Exercises/Scales:

Pieces:

Other important areas of focus including: Sight-reading, Music Theory, Aural, Listening

The boxes below are to record the number of minutes practice you do each day:

Monday	Tuesday	Wednesday	Thursday	Friday	Saturday	Sunday

Lesson Notes

Lesson date:

In our lesson today, we worked on the following:

Key things to practise this week
Exercises/Scales:

Pieces:

Other important areas of focus including: Sight-reading, Music Theory, Aural, Listening

The boxes below are to record the number of minutes practice you do each day:

Monday	Tuesday	Wednesday	Thursday	Friday	Saturday	Sunday

Lesson Notes

Lesson date:

In our lesson today, we worked on the following:

Key things to practise this week
Exercises/Scales:

Pieces:

Other important areas of focus including: Sight-reading, Music Theory, Aural, Listening

The boxes below are to record the number of minutes practice you do each day:

Monday	Tuesday	Wednesday	Thursday	Friday	Saturday	Sunday

Lesson Notes

Lesson date:

In our lesson today, we worked on the following:

Key things to practise this week
Exercises/Scales:

Pieces:

Other important areas of focus including: Sight-reading, Music Theory, Aural, Listening

The boxes below are to record the number of minutes practice you do each day:

Monday	Tuesday	Wednesday	Thursday	Friday	Saturday	Sunday

Printed in Great Britain
by Amazon

29110881R00059